© Aladdin Books Ltd 1990

*First published in
the United States in 1990 by*
Gloucester Press
387 Park Avenue South
New York NY 10016

ISBN 0-531-17197-3

Library of Congress Catalog
Card No: 89-81597

Printed in Belgium

The publishers would like to acknowledge that
the photographs reproduced within this book
have been posed by models or have been
obtained from photographic agencies.

Design David West
             Children's Book Design
Editor Margaret Fagan
Researcher Cecilia Weston-Baker
Illustrator Banjo Illustration

*The author, Brian Gardiner, is an atmospheric scientist.
He works for the British Antarctic Survey and was one
of the three scientists who discovered the hole in the ozone
layer.*

*The consultants: Dr John Becklake is Head of the Department
of Engineering, Science Museum, London, England. Mrs Sue Becklake
has a degree in Science and has written many books for
children on space. Dr Alan Morton, PhD, is curator of
Modern Physics at the Science Museum, London.*

ENERGY DEMANDS

BRIAN GARDINER

GLOUCESTER PRESS
London · New York · Toronto · Sydney

CONTENTS

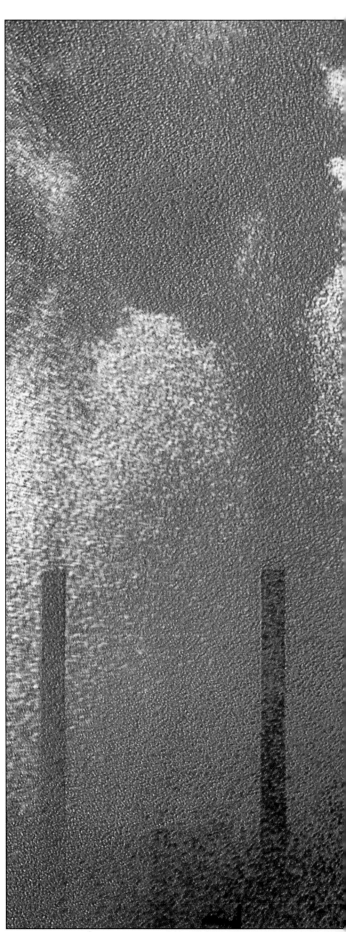

▷ Coal-fired power stations supply huge
amounts of energy, but they do have drawbacks. Their pollution adds to the problems of
acid rain and the greenhouse effect.

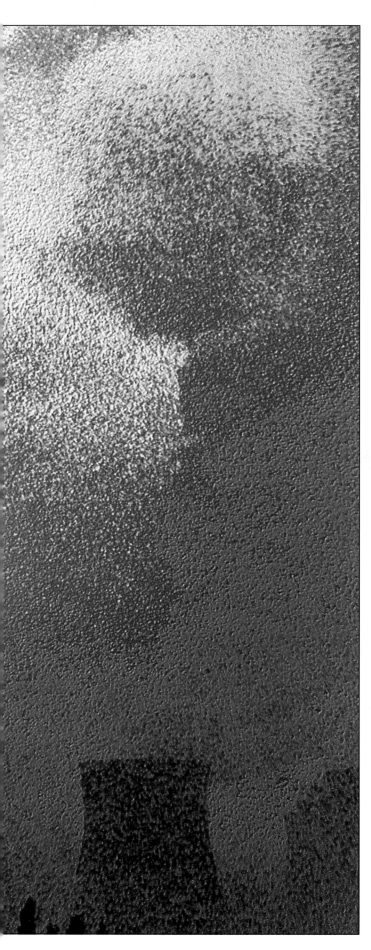

INTRODUCTION

The importance of an energy supply only comes home to us when it fails – in a power cut, or in a car that runs out of gasoline. At other times we take energy for granted and make huge demands on our energy supply. But where does it come from, and can it be relied on to keep coming in the future? Increasing environmental awareness has raised another question: how much pollution does each source of energy cause?

The answers are interesting and alarming. In the case of gasoline, the energy comes from a dwindling supply of oil, and it causes many pollution problems. Some of these can be tackled by changing car exhaust systems. This will reduce the emission of nitrogen oxides, carbon monoxide, and unburned gasoline, making city air cleaner and healthier to breathe. But it cannot prevent the emission of carbon dioxide, which is always produced by the combustion of any fossil fuel – coal, oil, or gas. Carbon dioxide is a major factor in the greenhouse effect, which leads to climate change. This fact is now used as an argument for more nuclear power stations. We are in a trap: to avoid climatic catastrophe we must find a solution to radio-active waste and minimize the risk of nuclear accidents. Or is there a third alternative?

Solar, wind, wave and other renewable energy sources have potential advantages. These last indefinitely without ruining the climate. But opponents claim that renewable energy can never supply more than a few percent of our requirements. So the battle lines are drawn in a three-cornered fight: fossil, nuclear, and renewable. We have no time to lose in resolving these questions. The atmosphere is changing faster than ever before; we are wasting fossil fuels at an alarming rate; and we have still not decided what to do with radioactive waste.

Chapter One

ENERGY NEEDS

Energy is essential for survival. Careful planning will be needed to ensure future supplies. Energy sources vary in cost and convenience. No single method can provide for all our needs.

Throughout the world, human beings need a supply of energy every day. The demand for energy has grown dramatically during the last 100 years, as the modern industrialized world consumes vast amounts of energy to maintain its high standard of living. Our stocks of oil and natural gas are already in danger of running out. To rely on coal would make matters worse because it contributes to the greenhouse effect, which will cause unpredictable climate changes. Other sources of energy can solve the problem, but only if they are studied and developed without delay. This will mean difficult choices.

△ What will happen when the oil runs out?

Food energy
The most vital part of our energy requirement is food. Chemical energy, coming from food during digestion, provides power for the muscles and warmth for the blood. The energy in food comes from sunlight. Vegetables, fruit, grain and rice get their energy by the chemical process called photosynthesis, in which green leaves transform carbon dioxide and water into stored energy in the form of carbohydrates by using the sun's light energy. In eating meat, or milk, or eggs, we are getting energy from the grass or other food which the animal ate.

△ Careful planning ensures a steady supply.

How to make stocks last

When a source of food energy is in danger of running out, it makes sense to reduce consumption and plan ahead to avoid a sudden shortage. For that reason, marine biologists study the life cycles of plankton and fish in order to calculate the amount that can safely be caught each year without depleting the stocks. This amount is called the "sustainable yield." It should be possible to go on indefinitely, harvesting that quantity each year. This idea of a sustainable yield is well understood in the fishing industry.

If food were our only energy requirement, the future would be easier to plan. But human beings need energy for many other purposes. In looking at other forms of energy, it will be helpful to bear in mind the concept of the sustainable yield. Can we take energy from a river indefinitely? At first sight it looks possible, but some rivers carry so much silt that they will clog within a few years if a dam is built for a hydroelectric power station. What is the sustainable yield of oil? Burning oil until stocks are exhausted is somewhat like hunting whales to extinction. However, there is a difference. Whale stocks can recover if whaling is banned in time, but oil supplies will not recover: once burned they are gone for good. To ensure long-term survival we need energy sources that will not run out.

In the sea, the sunlight is used by the tiny plants called phytoplankton, which capture the sun's energy by photosynthesis and provide food for the fish. Naturally this puts a limit on the quantity of fish in the sea, and this in turn may affect the size of the fishermen's catch.

Fishing fleets are indirectly harvesting the solar energy which falls on the sea. If they persistently catch fish faster than they can be replaced, then the fish stocks will run out, and the fishing industry will collapse. The same is true of whales. In the Antarctic they are now facing the threat of extinction.

Everyone needs energy

Even in the least developed parts of the world, people need energy at home. A subsistence farmer in central Africa works under the intense heat of the tropical sunshine. But when the sun goes down, the clear skies allow the ground to cool quickly. His family needs energy for cooking, and for warmth and light in the evening. They will burn wood, or dried dung from their animals. Farmers who grow enough food to sell can buy kerosene (paraffin) for a lamp.

In the industrialized world, we demand energy not only for cooking, lighting and heating, but also for the machines in factories and homes, from power drills to washing machines, from steel presses to television sets. Wherever goods and people are to be transported, fuel is required for cars, trucks, railways, ships and aircraft. All of these activities use massive amounts of energy: the United States, with 5 percent of the world's population, uses 25 percent of the energy produced. Fifteen percent of the world's population lives in India, but they only consume 3 percent of the energy produced.

Choice of energy sources

It would be easier if one type of energy could provide all our needs, but that is impossible. Nuclear energy is not available to the subsistence farmer in Ethiopia, and the wood fuel which his wife uses to cook their meals would not be much use for running a television set. A fuel that is cheap and convenient for one purpose may not suit another.

For homes, stores, offices and factories, it is cheaper to make electricity in a large power station and distribute it by cables to where it is needed. Some equipment must have electricity – like televisions and computers. The manufacture of technological appliances also demands energy. In fact it takes more energy to make a car than to run it for a year. The choice of fuel always comes down to a question of cost and convenience.

△ Two million people rely on wood for their fuel.

△ A coal-fired power station works best if it is kept running steadily.

△ In a Welsh mountain this hydroelectric storage system starts up in seconds.

Which fuel for power stations?

When it comes to running a power station to generate electricity, the obvious thing to do is find the cheapest fuel and use it. The trouble is that people want a lot of electricity before dinner (for their electric stoves) and in the evening (television, lights, electric baseboard heat, water heaters), but very little at night when hardly anything is switched on.

One of the cheapest fuels for generating electricity is coal, but it takes many hours to bring a coal-fired power station up to full blast, and it would be uneconomic to keep extra power stations running day and night just to cope with mealtimes. The electricity companies therefore rely on coal and nuclear stations running flat out for the "base load," and start up oil-fired stations and gas turbines quickly during the hours of peak electricity demand.

Keeping a wide selection

Each energy source has its particular merits, in convenience, cost, or speed of response. There are also political considerations: it is often worthwhile to import fuel from abroad, but a nation may prefer not to become dependent on others for energy, in case they put the price up too much or cut off supplies altogether during periods of international tension.

Improving efficiency
Surplus energy from coal and nuclear stations can be stored overnight by pumping water up into an artificial lake. Next day, during a television commercial, thousands of people switch on electric kettles for a cup of coffee. Valves open in seconds, releasing a cascade of water to drive the hydroelectric turbines.

7

Energy today

Most of the energy consumed today in the industrialized world comes from coal, oil and natural gas. These fossil fuels are the buried remains of plants and animals from millions of years ago. Unfortunately, the oil and gas are running out, and we dare not burn all the coal for fear of ruining the climate.

Even hydropower does not last forever. Hydroelectricity is generated at the base of an artificial waterfall constructed by building a dam across a river. Sometimes silt clogs up the river. Eventually there is not enough stored water to last through a dry spell and the generators stop.

In the developing countries, where most people cannot afford fossil fuels, energy for heating and cooking comes from plants and animals – biomass energy. Dried animal dung from the fields and wood from the forest are burned. Methane gas is generated from plant and animal waste materials. Wood fuel becomes scarce if trees are cut down faster than they can be replaced.

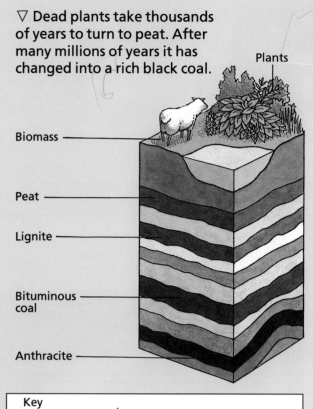

▽ Dead plants take thousands of years to turn to peat. After many millions of years it has changed into a rich black coal.

Plants

Biomass

Peat

Lignite

Bituminous coal

Anthracite

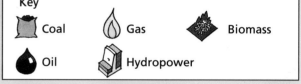

Key

Coal Gas Biomass

Oil Hydropower

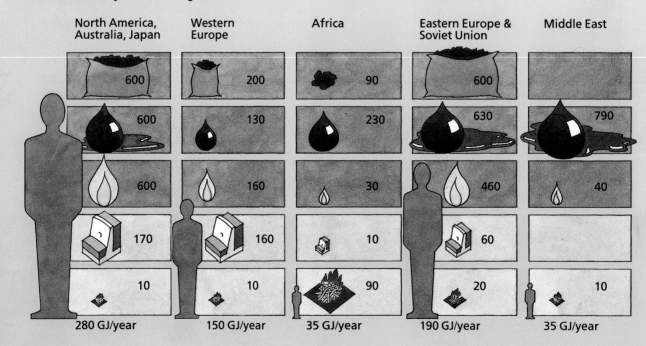

	North America, Australia, Japan	Western Europe	Africa	Eastern Europe & Soviet Union	Middle East
Coal	600	200	90	600	
Oil	600	130	230	630	790
Gas	600	160	30	460	40
Hydropower	170	160	10	60	
Biomass	10	10	90	20	10
	280 GJ/year	150 GJ/year	35 GJ/year	190 GJ/year	35 GJ/year

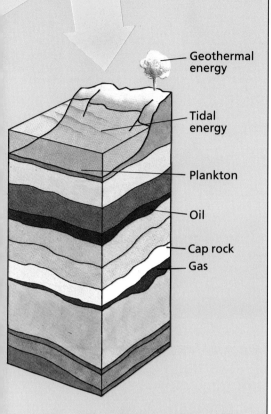

Geothermal energy

Tidal energy

Plankton

Oil

Cap rock

Gas

△ Fossil fuels can be found even beneath the sea bed. These deposits of oil and natural gas will be gone in a few decades.

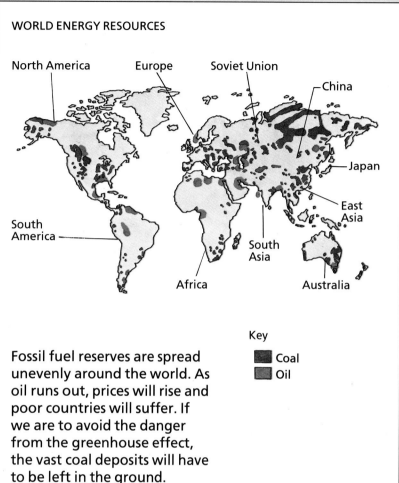

WORLD ENERGY RESOURCES

North America   Europe   Soviet Union   China

Japan

East Asia

South America

South Asia

Africa   Australia

Key
■ Coal
■ Oil

Fossil fuel reserves are spread unevenly around the world. As oil runs out, prices will rise and poor countries will suffer. If we are to avoid the danger from the greenhouse effect, the vast coal deposits will have to be left in the ground.

South America	China	South Asia
10	400	130
320	100	120
70	10	40
50	20	20
80	40	150
60 GJ/year	25 GJ/year	15 GJ/year

◁ **ENERGY STORE**
Some nations use more resources than others. The diagram (left) shows how much coal, oil and gas each region produces per year (in millions of tons of oil equivalent), and how much hydropower and biomass fuel they consume. People in rich countries use far more energy than the poorest, as shown by the size of the person standing next to each region. Note how the Middle East produces oil for use elsewhere, and how South Asia depends on wood fuel.

Chapter Two

FINITE FUELS

Fossil fuels are running out. By contributing to the greenhouse effect they will alter the climate. Substituting nuclear power means confronting the problems of radioactive waste disposal.

Most of the energy consumed in the developed world comes from coal, oil, natural gas and uranium. These fuels have served us well for many years, but they are now in trouble. The first problem is that they are all in finite supply, with the crisis already in sight for oil and gas. Uranium is consumed in nuclear power stations and there is no way of ever making it again. The other problem is the greenhouse effect. Coal, oil and gas all contribute to it, while uranium has its own long-term difficulties. These problems cannot be left for future generations to solve; they must be faced up to now.

△ Satellite mapping reveals uranium deposits in Utah. Will the world's uranium ever run out?

Fossil fuels
Coal, oil and natural gas are the buried remains of vegetation and other organisms which flourished on the Earth in ancient geological periods of the Earth's development. The energy in these "fossil fuels" comes from the accumulated sunshine collected by prehistoric plants while they were growing. Gradually the slow processes of rock formation have squeezed and transformed the organic substances in these plants into the coal, oil and natural gas that we now take for granted. The fossil fuels took many millions of years to form, but we are now squandering them so fast that future supplies are already in danger. If we continue to burn them as we have in the past, all the most valuable reserves will be consumed during the next few generations of the human race. If this happens, our descendants will surely accuse us of irresponsibility.

Fossil fuels (and uranium) are used

△ Power stations waste two-thirds of the energy in the fuel they burn.

throughout the world in the power stations that generate electricity. The huge stations that provide most of our electricity all work on the same principle. They burn the fuel to make heat, which is used to boil water into steam. The pressure of the steam turns the blades of a rotating metal fan called a turbine, which turns the shaft of the electric generator. Now the whole idea of a power station is to extract the energy from the fuel and send that energy out into the public electricity network. Unfortunately, the process of making electricity from a hot fuel is very inefficient. Only about a third of the energy leaves the power station as electricity. The other two-thirds end up in the cooling system of the power station, and are entirely wasted. In fact, the system is carefully designed to get rid of this waste heat immediately, as the turbines will not work properly if surplus heat is allowed to build up. Power stations are often built near the coast so that they can use sea water to carry away the waste heat. Inland stations

use a river or enormous cooling towers in which the waste heat is carried upward in a stream of warm, moist air.

Why are power stations so inefficient?
The low efficiency of power stations is an example of the important difference between heat energy and work energy. Anything involving movement or rotation means work, so it includes everything on wheels, washing machines, fans and pumps. Given some work energy, it is easy to convert all of it into heat, for example vehicle brakes and power drills both become hot when used. But the reverse process is more difficult. The heat in the brakes cannot easily be used to get the vehicle moving again!

In fact, it is impossible to convert heat completely into work energy, even in the most efficient engines. This is true of all heat engines, from cars to power stations. Engineers are up against a fundamental law of nature which limits the efficiency of the conversion, although it can be improved by raising the temperature of the hot parts while keeping the cold end as cool as possible. In practice, the upper limit is determined by the tendency of the metal components to deform, corrode and melt at very high temperatures. Power engineers have struggled hard for many years to design power stations that will capture more than a third of the energy from the fuel and transfer it to the electricity network, and in some cases they have succeeded in turning more than 40 percent of the fuel energy into electricity.

Can the waste heat be used?

In some countries, the surplus heat from power stations is put to good use by heating buildings close to the power station. Steam is piped around the streets from the cool end of the turbines. Unfortunately, although the output steam from a power station carries huge quantities of heat, its temperature is not high enough for a district heating system. (It is rather like putting too much cold water into a bath. All the heat that was in the hot water tank is now in the bath, but the water is tepid.) When the power station is adjusted for hotter output steam, it becomes less efficient at producing electricity. The plan works well if the town and its local power station are designed and built together. It is then called a CHP system (Combined Heat and Power), and has been very successful in Sweden, where the cold winter climate favors it.

Coal: the fuel of the Industrial Revolution

It is easy to forget that the modern industrialized world was built on the energy of coal. Before the nineteenth century water power and animal power were used. Metals were smelted in ovens fired by charcoal, which is made by slowly cooking wood until the moisture and gases have been driven off. In a furnace, charcoal will burn hot

△ Open-cast mining.

enough to melt iron and copper. Even today, Brazil uses several million tons of charcoal a year to manufacture steel. Europe, on the other hand, simply did not have enough trees to make charcoal on the vast scale required for heavy industry. The breakthrough came in 1709 when coke was first used in a blast furnace for making iron. Coke is made from coal, so it was no longer necessary to use wood. With iron and coal it was possible to use steam engines to pump water from the coal workings, and mine deeper to reach the vast underground reserves of coal. The nineteenth century saw an unprecedented growth in energy consumption during the industrialization of Great Britain. More coal was burned in the two years 1899 and 1900 than during the whole century between 1700 and 1800.

Mining has always been a dirty and dangerous business, not only for the miners but also on the surface, where subsidence and landslip have caused many accidents. In Britain, a collapsing spoil heap containing a sludge of wet coal dust and ash engulfed a school in 1966, killing those inside. The waste from coal mines can ruin the appearance of the countryside, especially in the vast surface mines of the United States, where the coal is uncovered by stripping off the overlying rock with excavators towering 328 feet high. A large expense is now required to mitigate any environmental insult from this process.

Coal does not burn cleanly. Smoke from coal fires was responsible for the infamous London smogs of the 1950s in which thousands of people died from respiratory diseases. Nowadays, coal has to compete with the other fossil fuels, and more attention is being given to the pollutants which can escape from coal-fired power stations.

Burning coal in power stations
The generation of electricity from coal is no easy task, as huge quantities of materials have to be processed continuously. The coal is crushed to a fine powder, which floats and burns white-hot in the stream of air as it rises through the furnace. The heat is collected by steam pipes in the furnace itself and in the hot exhaust gases as they rise up to the flue. The high-pressure steam then goes to the turbines to generate electricity.

About 6,000 tons of exhaust gases rush up the flue every hour, containing 1,200 tons of carbon dioxide, 200 tons of steam and about 30 tons of finely powdered ash. This fly ash contains sulfur oxides, arsenic and other environmental contaminants. If it falls to earth, it will pollute the ground-water. But extracting half a ton of ash every minute from a stream of hot, wet, corrosive gases is not easy. To make matters worse, the sulfur in the coal produces several tons of sulfur dioxide (SO_2) every hour, which can cause acid rain downwind of the power station. Filters can catch the ash, but not the SO_2. Water sprays mixed with powdered limestone deal with both, but produce 400 tons an hour of liquid sludge.

△ Industrial pollution in Brazil.

△ Damage to trees in Germany.

Acid rain
If sulfur dioxide from coal-fired power stations is allowed to escape, it will eventually land on the ground or dissolve in the rain. It is the ideal ingredient for making sulfuric acid which harms plants, animals and fish. Acid rain may land in another country, causing international anger.

Oil and natural gas

The other fossil fuels, oil and natural gas, burn more cleanly than coal, leaving no solid waste. They are more portable, easier to use, and can be turned on and off quickly. In fact, oil is so convenient that nearly all road and air transportation throughout the world now depends on gasoline, diesel, and kerosene.

There are, however, two major hitches. The first is that the largest oil reserves are in the Middle East. Consequently, much of industrialized Western Europe and North America depend for their energy on a politically unstable region of the world. The other hitch is that the oil reserves will run out in a few decades if we keep on using them at the present rate. North Sea oil has already passed its peak, and the vast North American oil fields are no longer able to keep up with the increased demand in the United States. The price of oil can therefore be set artificially by the countries who have more oil than they need. Predicting the future price of oil means forecasting the behavior of the Organization of Petroleum Exporting Countries (OPEC).

The future of oil could be extended by extracting it from tar sands and oil shales, but this is an expensive process as it takes many tons of these rocks to produce one ton of oil.

The same can be said of natural gas, which often comes out of oil wells together with the oil. Natural gas was once regarded as a nuisance by oilmen, and was flared off to get rid of it. Now it is often saved, and is also extracted on its own from gas fields. Natural gas has the advantage that it can be piped into the home, but oil packs more energy into a smaller volume, and is therefore more suitable for transportation.

Do fossil fuels have a future?

Until a few years ago, the prospects for fossil fuels looked good. Improvements in efficiency and pollution control would make them more acceptable to the public for the foreseeable future, and as the oil and gas ran out, synthetic liquid fuels from coal would provide for our transportation needs for hundreds of years. The vast unexplored deposits of coal which are believed to exist in China, the Soviet Union, and the United States, would enable us to leave to our descendants the problem of what to use after coal.

△ Laying a pipeline.

▽ Flaring off natural gas from an oil rig.

But all that has now changed. It is no longer just a question of finding enough fossil fuels to satisfy our insatiable demand. We now have to consider the effect that they are having on the atmosphere, the greenhouse effect, which will alter climate and affect the growth of food crops. In the past we have overcome many objections to fossil fuels by introducing sophisticated controls and techniques, but this new difficulty cannot be overcome. It lies in the very structure of the fossil fuels themselves.

△ Food crops are sensitive to climate.

The greenhouse effect

Governments throughout the world are now concerned about the greenhouse effect. So how does it work? The world would soon overheat if it was not able to get rid of the energy which it receives every day from the sun. Infrared radiation is continuously leaving the ground on its way to space, carrying off the excess heat. Carbon dioxide (CO_2) in the atmosphere captures some of this heat and sends it back to warm the Earth again.

The greenhouse effect
Infrared rays are invisible to our eyes, but they play a vital role in carrying heat off to space from the surface of the Earth. On its journey up through the atmosphere, an infrared ray may be captured by a carbon dioxide molecule. It is soon released again, but in a random direction. It has forgotten which way it was going, and may arrive at the Earth, warming it up. Like glass in the greenhouse, the carbon dioxide has trapped the heat.

A delicate balance
Without the greenhouse effect the Earth's surface would be at least 100 degrees Fahrenheit colder than it is. So if the greenhouse effect is so necessary, what is there to fear? The concentration of carbon dioxide in the atmosphere has been increasing dramatically since the Industrial Revolution. To make matters worse, new chemicals add to the greenhouse effect, for example the chlorofluorocarbons (which damage the ozone layer), and methane and nitrous oxide. More CO_2 is produced when trees are burned in the tropical forests. The oceans absorb about half of the extra CO_2, but cannot cope with any more than that.

15

Altering the climate

By the year 2030 the greenhouse effect will probably be equivalent to twice the old concentration of CO_2. There will undoubtedly be drastic changes in climate as the greenhouse effect warms the Earth's surface, but scientists using the best computers in the world are still unable to predict exactly what these changes will be. Rainfall, drought, temperatures and storms will all be affected, especially in the regions that we now depend on for growing grain. Tropical insects and diseases may spread to temperate latitudes, and coastal regions may be flooded as the oceans warm and expand. *Can we afford to take risks with our future by continuing to pour carbon dioxide into the atmosphere?*

△ Exhaust steam from a geothermal borehole on North Island, New Zealand.

△ When the climate changes, crops fail and food becomes scarce.

Geothermal energy

One alternative source of energy to fossil fuel has been in use for thousands of years; geothermal heat. Deep down, the Earth is very hot, owing to the natural radioactivity in the rock. This provides a source of energy as the heat leaks slowly to the surface. In some parts of the world, mostly in volcanically active regions, hot springs and geysers have been tapped to provide district heating. In principle it should be possible to create geothermal wells by drilling holes in suitable hot rock formations and extract endless free energy for heating or electricity generation. Unfortunately, the amount of energy leaking to the Earth's surface is negligible. It is useful only in a few locations where variations in the Earth's crust have allowed the heat to build up near the surface.

Geothermal energy is neither clean nor renewable, but it will continue to be a valuable energy source in places like Iceland and New Zealand for the foreseeable future. And it does not add to the greenhouse effect. To find a buried fuel which will not increase carbon dioxide in the atmosphere,

16

and yet produce enough convenient energy where we want it, we must turn to uranium.

Nuclear Energy

Controversy over the future of nuclear energy has now reached a crisis. Some people see it as the best long-term replacement for fossil fuels. Others point to the environmental hazard of radioactive waste and the high cost of dismantling derelict nuclear power stations safely. Building new nuclear power stations has also become prohibitively expensive. Only governments can afford to invest in them. Some countries have decided never to build another one, while other countries have plans for many more.

△ A nuclear power station in Austria.

Uranium fuel
Out of every 1,000 atoms of natural uranium, 7 are U-235 and 993 are U-238. (See glossary.) Today's reactors rely on the rare U-235 atoms. If the U-238 could be put to good use by converting it into plutonium fuel (Pu-239), reserves of uranium would last 50 times longer. created from U-238.

The energy in a nuclear power station comes originally from uranium which has been extracted from a processed ore taken from a uranium mine. It will not last forever. Sooner or later the uranium mines will run out, just like coal mines and oil wells.

In a conventional power station burning coal or oil, the energy comes from the chemical reactions between carbon, hydrogen and oxygen atoms. These reactions involve the electrons which surround the nucleus of each atom, but not the nucleus itself. The end products, carbon dioxide and water, do not contain as much energy as the original materials, and the surplus energy is available for us to use. In a nuclear reactor, the energy is obtained by splitting the nucleus of a uranium atom, usually into two large pieces and a few neutrons – a process called fission. The fragments do not contain as much energy as the original nucleus, and again we benefit from the surplus energy.

How a reactor works

Inside a nuclear reactor there are four vital materials: the fuel rods, the moderator, the coolant and the control rods. All four are to be found in the reactor. The fuel is uranium. When a U-235 nucleus is split inside a nuclear reactor, it produces two or three fast (very energetic) neutrons. The idea is to get one of these neutrons to split another atom of U-235 to keep the chain reaction going. These fast neutrons are slowed down as they pass through the moderator (usually water or graphite) because slow neutrons are more efficient at splitting U-235. The control rods (typically made of boron) capture the other neutrons before they can split a nucleus. In this way the chain reaction is controlled. The energy of the neutrons heats the reactor up, and the coolant carries the heat away to the steam generators to make steam for the turbines.

△ Storage area for metal drums containing radioactive nuclear waste.

△ Experimental dumping ground for nuclear waste in a salt cavern.

Radioactive waste

Low-level radioactive waste such as contaminated clothing and laboratory equipment can be buried in trenches or dumped at sea. But the spent fuel rods from a nuclear reactor contain high-level waste which will be untouchable for thousands of years. It could be encased in glass and concrete and buried deep underground, but even the toughest glass changes its crystal structure gradually. If it became brittle, the radioactive material could leak out and percolate into the water supply. To avoid this, geologists search for suitable areas where the rock is free of cracks.

Radioactive waste

Before it goes into the reactor, a uranium fuel rod is only mildly radioactive, and can be handled easily. But when the spent fuel rods are removed after a year or more in the reactor, they are lethally radioactive. Some countries send their spent fuel rods in special containers to a reprocessing factory which extracts the unused uranium, and also any plutonium. The rest of the material is highly radioactive and remains so for thousands of years.

The most promising way of disposing of this waste in the future is to encase it in blocks of glass and bury them in stable rock layers. In the meantime, the accumulated waste is stored in secure buildings. One of the most awkward objections to nuclear power is this expensive legacy for which acceptable solutions will have to be achieved by future generations.

△ On the anniversary of the Chernobyl tragedy, relatives remember the victims.

Nuclear accidents
The infamous reactor accidents at Three Mile Island in the United States and Chernobyl in the Soviet Union were caused by loss of coolant fluid and errors of judgment by human operators. The cores of these reactors are still lethally radioactive.

△ Experimental fast breeder reactor.

A safe solution to our energy problems?
As nuclear power does not produce carbon dioxide, it looks like a possible solution to the problem of the greenhouse effect. Unfortunately, at the present rate, the reserves of U-235 will only last about 100 years. If nuclear power were expanded to take over a significant part of world energy production, the U-235 would be gone even before the oil had run out. Uranium reactors can make a contribution to the needs of a few countries, but they cannot supply the world's energy. However, there is a way around this difficulty.

Fast breeder reactor
In today's uranium reactors, the amount of plutonium produced from U-238 is very small. But a reactor can be designed specifically to optimize the production of Pu-239. By using only fast neutrons, it is possible to consume fuel and at the same time convert more U-238 into fresh plutonium fuel. In this way, extra plutonium is bred which can be used to fuel other fast breeder reactors.

As usual, there is a price to pay: the concentrated fuel in a fast breeder reactor produces such an intense heat that it has to be cooled by molten sodium. Two experimental fast breeder reactors are operating in the United States: the Fast Flix Test Facility (FFTF) in Richland, and the Experimental Breeder Reactor II (EBR II) in Idaho Falls, Idaho.

Nuclear fusion
In the distant future it may be possible to obtain power from water by the process of nuclear fusion. This uses the energy left over when one nucleus joins another. However, it only works at the temperatures found inside a hydrogen bomb, and has proved to be a nightmare to control. It will be a long time before it can be put to any beneficial use.

Chapter Three

SUSTAINABLE FUELS

There are many sources of energy which will last forever. All have difficulties, but each has a contribution to make. Some methods are in use already, and more are on the way.

At first glance, the future of energy seems to be a stark choice between heaps of radioactive waste and drastic climate change. And since we do not have nuclear cars, it looks as if we might have to put up with both. But all the fuels so far considered will eventually run out. Perhaps the solution can be found in the renewable sources of energy – water, wind and sun – from which, like prudent fishermen, we can extract a "sustainable yield" of energy forever.

△ Egyptian villagers collect water from the Nile River.

Hydro- and tidal power

Large volumes of water, descending to a turbine generator far below, can indeed offer an efficient source of electricity. As there is no heat engine involved, nearly all the energy goes into the electricity supply. In some parts of the world, hydroelectric power is plentiful. Canadians refer to their electricity supply simply as "the hydro."

There are possibilities for new hydroelectric projects in Africa and South America, but in the world as a whole there is only limited scope for increasing the contribution presently made by hydroelectric power. There is public opposition to new dams and artificial lakes for environmental reasons; one large project in India has been fought for more than 30 years. Interrupting the flow of a river can have unexpected results. Silt builds up behind the dam, steadily reducing the depth of the lake. What looks like an endless source of energy will eventually get

△ Plentiful water at a hydroelectric dam.

clogged up. There are downstream effects too. When the Aswan Dam was completed, Egyptian farmers ran short of irrigation water, and their Mediterranean fishing industry collapsed because the nutrients for the fish were no longer being washed down the Nile River.

Energy can also be obtained from the tides by building a barrier across a tidal channel, but the future potential for world energy needs is very small. There are only four suitable areas in the world: the Bay of Fundy in Canada, the Severn Estuary in Great Britain, the Sea of Okhotsk east of the Soviet Union, and La Rance in northwest France.

The only significant tidal power station in the world is at La Rance. Its peak output, 240 MW, is smaller than the continuous output of a typical coal or nuclear station. In any case, a tidal barrier can interfere with fisheries and the habitats of water birds, and may also cause a health hazard by preventing the flow of river pollution to the sea.

Energy from the waves

A much more promising, but as yet undeveloped, method of harnessing the power of water is to use the energy of ocean waves. An advancing wave carries with it the accumulated energy which it has collected from the wind on its journey across the ocean. This has stimulated engineers to design a wide variety of machines that could convert the wave energy into electricity.

Everything has been suggested, from hinged rafts and flexible air bags to nodding metal ducks, bobbing buoys and tanks with flaps. All the devices attempt to take the motion of the waves and use it to turn a turbine, either directly or by compressing air or water in a tube leading to the turbine.

So far, the types which are designed to float in the sea have not gone past the experimental stage, but a land-based system successfully delivered electricity for four years in Norway. This design consists of a 60 feet high cylinder built on the rocky shore. Each wave rises inside the cylinder, pushing the air up to turn a turbine at the top. The turbine is cleverly designed to continue rotating in the same direction when the descending wave sucks the air back down. The fate of this generator points out the biggest problem facing the future of wave energy. During a particularly energetic storm in 1988 it was smashed to pieces by the very waves that it was designed to use.

However, it would be foolish to write off wave energy as a failure just because of one broken machine. Most of our modern engineering techniques started out in the early days with a sequence of costly mistakes and breakages. There is every prospect of better wave generators in the near future, and the scope is worldwide. Wave energy has hardly any drawbacks (fish breeding grounds might have to be protected) and it could make a significant pollution-free contribution to world energy needs in the future. New designs for wave stations will be produced, but they will all have to be engineered to resist the fury of the sea.

OTEC

In the calmer waters of the tropics, there is a rather different method of extracting energy from the ocean. Ocean Thermal Energy Conversion (OTEC) is a heat engine which takes energy from the warm surface waters of the sun-drenched tropical ocean. Every heat engine must have a cold side: the OTEC system pumps up cool water from a depth of about 1,640 feet. As even the tropical seas are not boiling, the turbine cannot use steam. Instead it is driven by ammonia which is evaporated by the warm water and condensed by the cool water.

As the temperature difference is small, OTEC is very inefficient at making electricity, so large quantities of water have to be pumped through the system. A 200 MW OTEC power station would need a flow of water as great as that of the Missouri River. Fortunately this "fuel" would be free, but sea water is also corrosive. This is a problem even for the mini-OTEC system which is being tested in Hawaii. OTEC is cumbersome and costly, but it has the advantage that its energy source is always available, unlike the wind and the sun.

△ Who can harness the power of the waves?

Solar energy

As most of our energy comes originally from the sun, it makes sense to capture it right away, rather than wait for nature to process it into fossil fuels. The simplest method is the flat-plate collector on the roof of a house.

Pipes on the plate carry water to and from the domestic hot water tank. Sunshine warms the plate, and heat is picked up by the water as it passes. A sheet of glass allows the sunshine in, but keeps the plate warm by preventing the escape of infrared radiation – this is a deliberate form of greenhouse effect.

The water will only warm up once the sun is high enough in the sky. On cloudy days and in winter a flat-plate collector may not provide quite enough energy for a full tank of hot water, but it can still help to reduce the bill for gas or electricity.

Naturally, solar collectors are popular in sunny countries. In Israel, an interesting development is the solar pond, which is certainly not suitable for swimming. To begin with, it is partly filled with very salty water and then a layer of fresh water is carefully poured on top. The sun shines through the water and heats a black absorbing layer at the bottom of the pond, which makes the deep water warm. Normally this warm water would rise to the top, but in the solar pond the saltiest, and therefore the densest, water is at the bottom, and no amount of heating will make it rise. In fact it would reach boiling point if the heat were not piped off to a heat engine to generate electricity. A 5 MW station is already under construction. For countries with plenty of spare land and sun, this may prove to be a cheap source of electric power on a grand scale.

△ Solar panels are more economical if designed into new houses from the start.

△ Tilting a solar power array to collect maximum energy from the sun.

23

Focusing the sunlight

The idea of focusing the sun's rays with mirrors has attracted a lot of attention, and some very large arrays have been built. The advantage is that high temperatures can be reached, which makes for efficient generation of electricity. The drawback is that the mirrors must all track the sun to keep it focused on the collector. These grand schemes were too costly to build and to maintain, and it has so far proved impossible to make them any cheaper.

A useful lesson has been learned from the many attempts to introduce solar stoves in developing countries. It was thought that women who had to walk long distances to gather firewood for cooking would surely welcome solar stoves, but they have not been a success. A solar stove is a bowl-shaped mirror four feet in diameter, which focuses the sun onto the cooking pot. Although they were designed to be cheap, many people could not afford them. But there were other problems, too. People wanted to cook in the evening, but the stoves worked best in the blistering heat of the midday sun. They were awkward to use, and it was very easy to be burned when leaning over to adjust the position of the pot on the stove.

Photovoltaic energy

Perhaps the most exciting prospect for the future is electricity from solar cells. The complications of heat engines, turbines, generators, air pollution and radioactive waste could possibly be avoided, if the price of solar cells could be brought down. A small electric voltage is produced when light shines on a solar cell. It does not have to be direct sunlight: cloudy daylight will work just as efficiently.

Solar cells are made from very pure silicon crystals. Silicon itself is cheap, as it is common in sand and rocks; the high cost lies in the processes of purifying and crystallizing the silicon. It may eventually be possible to make cheaper solar cells from amorphous silicon, which is not crystalline. Electricity from solar cells could then compete with power from fossil fuels. But there is a problem, and it applies to all forms of solar power. It is that solar energy is available only during the day, and there is not much daylight in winter when more power is needed for heating and lighting.

One way around this problem is to find another source of renewable energy which will still work in the dark, and especially in winter. Fortunately, there is one readily available: the wind.

△ An array of photovoltaic solar cells will produce electricity even in cloudy weather. They are often used in remote locations, but are still too expensive for general use.

△ A commercial wind energy farm in California.

Wind power

Throughout recorded history the power of the wind has been tamed and put to work by sailors, millers and farmers. Who knows how the history of the Americas would have turned out if there had been no wind to fill the sails of the European fleets? On land, the wind has pumped water to irrigate the fields, to drain them and to grind the harvested grain. In the growing controversy on environmental issues today, the image of the windmill represents for many people a desire to return to the simplicity of village life before the days of heavy industry and high technology.

But wind power has come a long way since the days of the jolly miller. Today's wind turbines owe more to the aircraft designer than to the sailmaker. At first sight, the modern wind turbine appears to work on the same principle as the traditional windmill: the wind pushes against each blade and forces it around. But closer inspection reveals a profound difference between the old and the new.

The old-fashioned windmill has flat sails, angled slightly to divert the wind. It is easy to see which way the sails will turn. Apart from the four-sailed mills of yesteryear, there are still many multibladed windmills in use, mostly for pumping irrigation water and for small-scale electricity generation in areas too remote to be reached by the national network. These multibladed windmills are also of the traditional design, with flat blades angled to the wind.

Airfoil wind turbines

The modern wind turbine works on a completely different principle. It is in fact a kind of flying machine, with blades like the wings of an aircraft. These are designed in an airfoil shape: thick and rounded at the leading edge, but with a sharp trailing edge, like a sheet of paper which has been folded over, but not yet pressed flat. To begin with,

25

the wind turbine behaves like a sail windmill, but once it gets up to full speed the blades are flying so fast that the airfoil lift provides all the energy. The blades of a traditional windmill usually move more slowly than the wind, but in a modern turbine the blade tips normally travel five to ten times as fast as the wind. This explains why energy can be taken from the whole of the circle swept out by the blades, even though they are so narrow: no part of the airstream is left alone for long.

Wind systems already in use

The narrowness of the blades, and the fact that only two or three are needed, means that wind machines can be made much larger than in the old days, without accumulating too much weight on the bearings. The most powerful wind turbines in the world have blades 100-130 feet long, and generate up to 4 MW of electrical power. However, big is not always best. The most successful projects are found in California, where a typical multimegawatt "wind farm" consists of more than 100 turbines, each supplying 50 to 100 kW to the public network at a commercially competitive price. Arrays of this sort are built in mountain passes where the wind is naturally channeled to a higher speed. Doubling the wind speed makes eight times as much power available, so windmills of any type tend to provide most of their energy during the windiest spells.

There is also a type of turbine that works for any wind direction. It is called the vertical-axis wind turbine, and rotates around a vertical pole. There are two versions: the egg beater, in which two curved airfoils rotate like back-to-back archery bows joined at the top and bottom; and the letter-H type, in which the airfoils are the vertical bars of the H. In both types of vertical-axis turbine, it is difficult to see how the turbine knows which way to turn,

or even why it should turn at all. In fact, it depends on the airfoil principle, which only works once it is moving, so it has to be given a push to get it started.

If the electric companies introduce wind power on a large scale in the near future, they will probably build arrays of horizontal-axis machines in particularly windy places. A large cluster of wind turbines can be noisy for those living nearby, but a more awkward side effect is television interference as the broadcast signal bounces off the blades. These objections could be overcome by siting the wind turbines in shallow offshore waters.

△ A three-bladed egg-beater wind turbine.

Biofuels

In the developing world, organic materials such as wood and dried dung are burned as fuel for heating and cooking. But there are other less obvious sources of organic fuel which have been suggested as future energy substitutes for gasoline and kerosene. The first is alcohol, which can be made from sugarcane, cassava and other crops. In Brazil, two million cars have been modified to run purely on ethyl alcohol instead of gasoline, and the other eight million cars use a mix of one part alcohol to four parts gasoline. This project was started when oil prices rose steeply in the 1970s, but since they have fallen again the alcohol is more costly to produce than gasoline.

Nevertheless, many countries would rather produce their own fuel than have to spend reserves of foreign currency on importing oil. There are plans in India to make methyl alcohol (methanol) from wood. If all the wood presently used for cooking in India could be put into methanol production, there would be no need for India to buy diesel oil for vehicles.

Cooking could then be done with biogas, the other organic fuel of the future. Waste materials from animals and agriculture are allowed to decay in a tank to produce a gas which contains mostly methane, plus some carbon monoxide and hydrogen. Biogas can be burned for heat, and is widely used in China and India. The sludge that comes out of the biogas tank is a better fertilizer than the animal dung that went in, and the process also kills farm pests and diseases.

In the industrialized world, biogas from decaying material in city garbage dumps gradually percolates to the surface. To avoid explosions the gas is collected and can be put to good use if there is a local need for industrial heat. Biogas production can also be worthwhile on farms, but not for individual houses in towns. Success with a biogas tank requires skillful control of the temperature and input mixture. In cold climates, even large-scale sewage works consume more energy than they recover from biogas.

△ A fuel tanker fills up with fuel alcohol at a distillery in Brazil. The alcohol comes from fermented sugarcane juice.

△ Beneath this lily pond in Thailand there is a biogas digester tank which converts organic waste into methane and fertilizer.

27

Future sources

To ensure a continuous supply of energy far into the future, new power systems must make use of energy sources that will not run out – sunlight, wind and waves. These techniques exist already, and some are in commercial use, but it will take years of expensive research to develop their full potential. The rich industrialized countries will have to help the others to convert to these sustainable energy methods. Once they are in widespread use, they will provide the energy to build better and cheaper systems. Without such help the under-developed nations will be forced to continue burning coal, and everyone will suffer as the climate changes. The sooner we invest in the future, the sooner the problem will be solved.

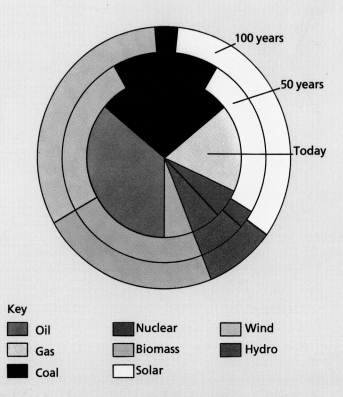

Key

■ Oil   ■ Nuclear   ■ Wind

□ Gas   ■ Biomass   ■ Hydro

■ Coal   □ Solar

△ **RUNNING OUT ?**
Today fossil fuels do most of the work. Nobody knows how the future will develop, but 100 years from now renewable energy will surely play a bigger role.

◁ **SOLAR**
Solar cells produce electricity directly from daylight, even in cloudy weather. New developments will make them cheaper.

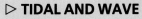

Sunlight

Electrical contacts

Negative silicon layer

Electrons flow out

Electrons flow in

Positive silicon layer

▷ **TIDAL AND WAVE**
Energy from the sea comes in two forms. This tidal barrier already exists, extracting energy as the tide ebbs and flows. The power in ocean waves is even greater and could be more productive, but it constantly threatens to destroy the machines built to tame it.

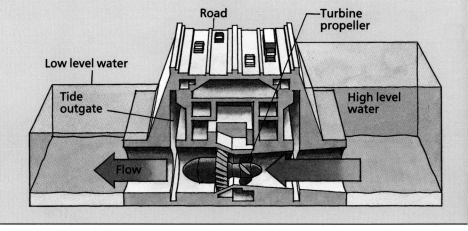

Road

Turbine propeller

Low level water

Tide outgate

High level water

Flow

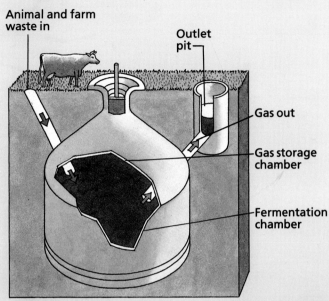

Animal and farm waste in

Outlet pit

Gas out

Gas storage chamber

Fermentation chamber

Steam up

Cold water down

Cracks through hot rocks

△ BIOMASS

This fermenter produces methane gas from the decay of crop waste material and animal dung. Methane can be burned like natural gas for cooking and heating purposes, or for local electricity generation.

▷ GEOTHERMAL

Deep in the Earth's crust the rocks are heated by natural radioactivity. In some places these hot rocks can be reached by boring holes. Energy can be then extracted for many years before the rocks cool down.

▽ WIND

Modern wind turbines are designed by aircraft engineers for maximum strength and efficiency. Wind farms are already operating commercially in California and Hawaii.

Fast breeder reactor

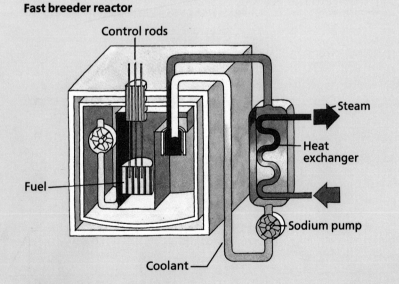

Control rods

Steam

Heat exchanger

Fuel

Sodium pump

Coolant

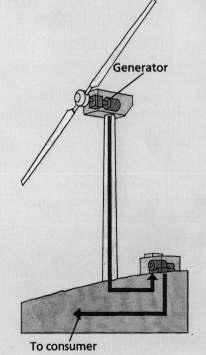

Generator

To consumer

△ NUCLEAR

Nuclear power could be made to last for hundreds of years, but not with today's reactors, which use less than one per-cent of the uranium. It would require development of Fast Breeder reactors on a grand scale. Unfortunately, they use plutonium, so the public may not accept this solution.

Chapter Four

FACING UP TO THE FUTURE

Energy conservation will reduce the drain on fossil fuels. Attitudes must change. Renewable energy provides a solution, but the developing countries will need assistance. Time is running out.

If the industrialized world is to keep up its present standard of living, some difficult decisions will have to be made. Consumption of fossil fuels will have to be drastically reduced if we are to avoid catastrophic changes in climate. New sources of energy must therefore be actively developed to take over from the fossil fuels. Fossilized attitudes will also have to go: new solutions will require fresh and imaginative thinking and a willingness to try out new ideas.

What can be done now?

Energy conservation is the first step. The introduction of cavity-wall insulation and other energy-saving measures in the home have a significant effect on a nation's power needs. Energy-efficient houses can be designed to capture solar energy by careful positioning of window areas and control of the airflow. The best of these houses stay warm in the winter and cool in the summer, with a fraction of the normal energy requirement. Industrial managers have already found that they can reduce electricity consumption and save money for their companies by including energy conservation in their factory planning.

△ The British nuclear fuel reprocessing plant. Governments worldwide are having second thoughts about the future of nuclear energy.

◁ Modern public transportation is clean and efficient.

Governments can help by giving companies tax rebates for the purchase of energy-saving equipment.

Cars can be manufactured to run on far less gasoline than at present, but they are very inefficient when compared to a full bus or train. Public transportation should be made more attractive to people who normally go everywhere by car.

But conservation is not enough. Energy is still needed in large quantities. In the long term it can only come from coal, nuclear and renewable energy sources. Coal can be made to last for centuries, but only by allowing an unacceptable concentration of carbon dioxide to build up in the atmosphere. Nuclear energy can also be developed for the future, but it will require fast breeder reactors which involve plutonium, and that could lead to an increase in the number of countries that can manufacture nuclear weapons. The waste from nuclear reactors remains radioactive for thousands of years.

Besides, nuclear energy is unsuitable for cars and buses since it produces nothing but electricity. To solve the greenhouse problem with nuclear energy alone would mean the introduction of a transportation fuel manufactured by electricity. Hydrogen is a possibility as it could be extracted from water by an electric current.

31

Investing in the future

Renewable energy sources have the tremendous advantage that they last forever, without adding pollution to the environment. But they are mostly in the earliest stages of development, and require considerable investment of time and money to make them economic. The sooner these methods are developed the better, as any delay simply means that more fossil fuels are being burned.

In the meantime, there are some stop-gap measures that would slow down the increase in carbon dioxide. Wherever possible, new power stations should be designed to make good use of their waste heat. Natural gas gives about twice as much energy per ton as coal, and produces less carbon dioxide per ton. Even oil is better than coal in this respect. There is therefore an advantage in converting from coal to oil or natural gas, while renewable sources are being developed to replace them.

Do we need to store energy?

To make full use of sun, wind and wave power, some method of energy storage will be required to cope with the times when the sea is calm, the wind has dropped, and the sun has gone down. It is already possible to store energy in caverns of compressed air, and by pumping water up to a reservoir lake. Chemical storage of energy would make it possible to use renewable sources for transportation fuel.

But there is no need to wait for progress in storage systems before installing wind power. Economic wind turbines exist already, and they can supply up to 5 percent of the power for a national electricity network, provided they are placed in a number of locations around the country. The variations in wind energy are then no worse than the variations in demand which the network already copes with. At the moment, many people regard wind turbines

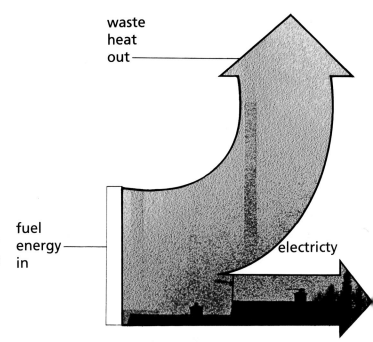

waste heat out

fuel energy in

electricty

Coal, oil, gas and nuclear power stations all lose two-thirds of the fuel energy as waste heat. Only one-third emerges as electricity.

△ Electricity pylons, like wind turbines, have their own stark beauty.

as ugly monsters. But we cannot face the future with inflexible attitudes. Provided care has been taken to deal with the environmental effects of wind energy, including noise, an array of modern windmills on the horizon could become a welcome sight. It may be the best way to avoid climatic change which would lead to food shortages throughout the world.

Understanding the needs of others

The energy problem cannot be solved by forcing people to give up their present way of life completely. Some people would like to return to the days when there were no factories, no cars and no air travel. Their energy needs are simple. But most people enjoy the advantages of modern living and have no desire to give them up. If future energy plans are to be successful they must therefore provide fuel for transportation. This may mean extracting oil from plants. It is already possible to design an engine to run on sunflower or peanut oil. The future of energy does not lie in one single source, but in a multitude of different sources, each with its own advantages.

To encourage progress in developing these new methods, governments across the world will have to agree on how to proceed. To protect the ozone layer, an international agreement was signed in 1987 to reduce the use of the chemicals that were causing the problem.

Such an agreement cannot work unless it includes most of the large countries in the world, such as China and India. But these countries are struggling to catch up with the standard of living enjoyed by the developed nations. If there is to be a similar international agreement to limit the burning of fossil fuels, China and India will need help. They depend on coal for much of their heavy industry and transportation.

△ Sunflowers can be harvested as a fuel crop. Vegetable oil is a renewable energy source.

▷ If standards of living are to improve, energy demands will have to be met.

Helping the Third World

Only the rich countries can afford to give the agricultural and industrial aid that will make it possible for the developing world to introduce fuel crops, wind turbines and solar power, all of which will help them to reduce their consumption of fossil fuels. It is no easy matter to organize such help, even when governments have put up the money. Many mistakes have been made in the past by forcing modern technology onto countries which did not have the facilities to maintain it. The solutions will have to be appropriate for the circumstances, skills and culture of each individual country.

The financial complications are very important. A farming community can easily be ruined by the introduction of a new crop from outside, if the farmers can no longer sell their old crop at a competitive price. A subsistence farmer may rely on cattle dung for his cooking fuel. If the landowner acquires a biogas generator from an international aid project, the poor farmer may be deprived of his fuel. The energy needs of the world can only be supplied by a careful mixture of new and old technology, designed to ensure that it will not create trouble in the long term. In choosing the way forward, we should always be looking for sustainability. There will be mistakes and disasters, as there always are with new endeavors. But one thing is certain: if we do nothing, the climate will change unpredictably and our precious reserves of buried fuels will keep on running out.

△ Solar-powered refrigerator for transporting vaccines by camel.

GLOSSARY

base load electricity which power stations must supply around the clock

biogas gas produced by the decay of biological waste

fast breeder a nuclear reactor which makes use of U-238 by converting it into Pu-239

fissile a material that will undergo nuclear fission, namely uranium -235, plutonium -239 and uranium -233

gas turbine a turbine turned by hot gases from a burner. If oil is burned, the power station does not need steam, and can be started up quickly.

HAWT horizontal-axis wind turbine

hydroelectric energy from falling water

moderator the material which slows down neutrons in a nuclear reactor

photosynthesis a process of green plants by which carbohydrates are formed from carbon dioxide and water in the air under the influence of light

photovoltaic electrical energy generated from sunlight

Pu-239 fissile isotope of plutonium containing 94 protons and 145 neutrons in each nucleus

subsistence farmer one with barely enough food for survival

turbine a fan of rotating blades forced around by the pressure of a liquid (such as water) or a gas (such as air or steam)

U-235 uranium with 92 protons and 143 neutrons. It releases energy when split.

U-238 uranium with 92 protons and 146 neutrons. It is useless until converted to Pu-239.

VAWT vertical-axis wind turbine

vitrification encasing radioactive waste in glass blocks

ENERGY UNITS

The international unit of **energy** is the joule

Each item in this list is a thousand times bigger than the one below:

EJ	exajoule	one day's energy for the world
PJ	petajoule	energy in an ocean tanker of oil
TJ	terajoule	energy in a road tanker of oil
GJ	gigajoule	energy in a car's gasoline tank
MJ	megajoule	food energy in a hamburger
KJ	kilojoule	energy to start an athlete running
J	one joule	energy of an apple dropping from a tree

The international unit of **power** is the watt. It means that energy is coming at the rate of a joule every second.

Each item in this list is a thousand times bigger than the one below:

PW	petawatt	solar power on Zaire at noon
TW	terawatt	world's electrical power output
GW	gigawatt	output of a large power station
MW	megawatt	heat from a large bonfire
KW	kilowatt	heat from an electric fire
W	one watt	power used by a small torch

INDEX

Photographic Credits:
Cover and pages 20, 21 and 22: Zefa; intro page and pages 7 top, 10, 18 left and right and 31: Science Photo Library; pages 6, 13 bottom and 17: Topham Picture Library; pages 7 bottom and 16 top: J. Allan Cash Library; page 11: Eye Ubiquitous; pages 12, 13 top and 34: Magnum Photos; pages 16 bottom, 19 bottom and 33 right: Rex Features; page 19 top: Frank Spooner Agency; pages 23 left, 25, 27, 32 and 33 left: Robert Harding Library; pages 23 right and 26: Sandia Laboratories; page 27: Panos Pictures.

RI